Gianni, Jan & Marcello Liscia

# WORKBOOK
# ATTITUDE

A question of personal attitude and values which are
lived and experienced

Illustrations:
Herman Reichold

Attitude is the fourth of five books in the D.R.E.A.M. of LEADERS®
publication series.

Bibliographic information of the The German National Library: The German National Library lists this publication in the German National Bibliography; detailed bibliographic data can be found on the website at http://dnb.dnb.de.

**1ˢᵗ edition 2018**

**Imprint**
**© 2018 Gianni, Jan & Marcello Liscia**

Layout, cover + worksheets: Franziska Eikel, Liscia Consulting
English translation by Ramey Rieger: doitwritetranslations@gmx.de

Text + Layout:
Biographiewerkstatt Böddeker
Ellerstraße 26 – 33100 Paderborn
Telephone: 05293 - 9327816

Print and publishers: : Books on Demand, Norderstedt
ISBN: 978-3-7528-5827-3

# Table of Contents

*"Making decisions is not difficult,*
*when you know what your values are."*[1]
Roy O. Disney (co-founder, Walt Disney Company)


**Dear Reader,**

We are immensely pleased that you are now holding our fourth workbook in your hands! With our workbooks and first publication, *D.R.E.A.M. of LEADERS®. Leadership is not an Illusion*, you have discovered a great deal about our understanding of leadership.

Or perhaps this book just fell into your hands and you're now wondering what this *D.R.E.A.M. of LEADERS®* could be? Well, for the past 15 years we have been accompanying people along their path to professional development. This is our passion, the most meaningful purpose we can imagine! Specializing in developing leaders, we originated the D.R.E.A.M. Formula[2]:

**D**  Dedication: Wholehearted commitment to mission, 24 hours a day
**R**  Responsibility: Assuming full responsibility for your decisions, for your staff and for yourself
**E**  Education: Ensuring you and your staff evolve
**A**  Attitude: Living and communicating your personal mindset (philosophy) and values
**M**  Motivation: Commitment as the foundation of all deeds

We usually work with our clients over an extended time period, getting to know one another quite well. Our mission is people work, building relationships of equal standing, which is reflected in the language we use. The D.R.E.A.M. Formula acronym can also be understood as a checklist, illustrating the self-

---

[1]  Unspecified quotes are taken from *Book of Quotations* (Bassermann-Verlag, 2013) or from digital quote collections.

[2]  D.R.E.A.M.-Formel® is a protected trademark owned by Liscia Consulting and registered with the German Patent and Trademark Office.

concept of a leader. It is how leadership can be understood and lived. This being a highly complex and multi-layered subject, our first publication, *D.R.E.A.M. of LEADERS®. Leadership is not an Illusion,* could only render a first impression of how we understand leadership.[1]

Going further into detail, we have subsequently published a workbook for each letter in the D.R.E.A.M. Formula acronym, providing more examples and worksheets at the end of each chapter for practical application of material learned. The workbook series is so conceived to be read and applied independent of our first book. The original chapters have retained their basic structure and are merely augmented by additional examples. Hence, reading the first book is not a prerequisite.

This workbook zeros in on the topic of attitude. Here, the values a leader embodies and communicates are of major significance. But we also should examine a leader's inner posture – for example, how he handles letting go and delegating; what to consider when leading teams of varying nationalities and ages and why happiness is an attituded issue, too.

We wish you enlightening reading and enjoyment filling out the worksheets!

---

[1]   To enhance readability, we have alternated masculine and feminine non-specific personal pronouns per chapter. Hence, in this context, we consider both genders gender-neutral and hope they are understood as such.

A ⌐

Attitude

| | |
|---|---|
| *LISCIA:* | What role do values play in your company? |
| *CEO:* | A huge one. |
| *LISCIA:* | What exactly is your approach to this topic? |
| *CEO:* | Our values are a part of our corporate culture and our employees are encouraged to uphold them. |
| *LISCIA:* | How do you know they do? |
| *CEO:* | It's an aspect of the annual talk and subsequent employee assessment. |
| *LISCIA:* | So, when values aren't upheld, the assessment results are less than rosy? |
| *CEO:* | Something like that. |
| *LISCIA:* | Do company values come into play before hiring a new employee? |
| *CEO:* | They've always been a part of onboarding. |
| *LISCIA:* | But not *before* hiring. |
| *CEO:* | No, not before hiring. *Before* hiring? |

## Values – The 9 Levels, à la Clare W. Graves

In our books *D.R.E.A.M. of LEADERS®. Leadership is not an Illusion* and *Workbook: Responsibility*, we have already touched upon varying values and principles. Principles should be enduring company attributes, consistently burning beacons for your employees' orientation, particularly during transitional processes.

Values, on the other hand, must be mutable, primarily determined by the organizational structure. The more hierarchical a company is structured, the more you will find values such as a sense of duty, obedience and/or discipline. Should the organizational structure change, these values must also be adapted to the new structure. Companies that endure for years or decades are distinguished by their ability to continuously change and adapt their values accordingly. Companies incapable of adapting are short-lived, quickly vanishing from the big picture.

In the 1960s, the U.S. American psychology professor Clare W. Graves and his students probed into the issue of value development, how they are upheld and how they change. The results of these studies culminated in the *Graves Value System*, depicting how individuals or entire systems (i.e. departments, companies, organizations) think and act.

Drawing on this model, Rainer Krumm, founder of the *9 Levels Institute for Value Systems* consulting firm, developed a tool with which the value systems of persons, groups and/or organizations could be measured and analyzed.

Several years ago, Rainer Krumm granted us certification to access and apply his scientifically validated model, which has more than proven its practical worth as well. The *9 Levels* do not, however, indicate leadership styles. They reveal the coherency between organizational structure and values.

As illustrating all levels would go beyond the scope of this publication, we have selected a choice few for clarification. *Level 2*, for example, encompasses enterprises with a patriarch at the top with all employees serving under him equally. There is but one executive level, commending values such as loyalty and obedience, where employees have little say-so.

In *Level 4* companies, the executive level is fanned out with, in some cases, a business management, a board of directors and various departmental managers for finances, quality control and/or personnel, etc. This organizational structure is quite stable, but stable can also be inflexible and cumbersome, as there is usually little or no communication between the various departments. Reports are sent only to the top. The United Nations is one example of a Level 4 organization. It upholds a very strict hierarchical structure, which is why decision-making is extremely sluggish and time-consuming.

A matrix organization is a *Level 6* structure and the first non-hierarchical arrangement. A matrix organization requires a high percentage of dialog and cooperation within horizontal hierarchies, demanding flexible leaders willing to listen to their employees' opinions. On the other hand, employees must be willing to actively invest their energies.

For this reason, a *9-Level analysis* of organizational structures is not only important, it is very illuminating. It substantiates that an employee embodying values of hierarchy and stability cannot be productive in a matrix structure. That would be a contradiction in itself. But a staff member open to dialog and cooperation needs the matrix structure to fully develop her potential. She would be wholly misplaced in a hierarchical company with a boss who turns a deaf ear to her ideas and input. When the surroundings are aligned with a person's values, it is immediately obvious how at home a worker feels. This is not due to his actual function in the business. His satisfaction is solely a result of the organizational structure within which he works. We often hear of employees driven to the limit because their values are not shared by their employer or superior. This constellation never bodes well.

Yet, there are situations that call for other tactics. Some time ago, during a coaching session, we spoke with a personnel officer who was thoroughly frustrated because his career had come to grinding halt. The *9-Level analysis* revealed him to be more consensus-oriented and cooperative. In his company, however, aggressive, demonstrative behavior was necessary to avoid being overlooked at promotion time. If you don't draw enough attention to yourself, the job goes to someone else. And precisely in the section of the *9-Level analysis* addressing aggressive, demonstrative behavior, the man had scored the lowest points. The coaching made clear he would have to step out of his comfort zone for a while; would have to temporarily act contrary to his values. Not for long, but long enough to serve his purpose. It was the only way to advance his career.

It is a rare company that grasps the direct interaction between organizational structure and values. When, say, the Catholic Church rests on conservative values, explicitly demanding their members and employees uphold them, it is clearly a contradiction when, at the same time, progressive cardinals at the Vatican Bank behave like hedge fund managers.

Thus, it is not possible to change the architecture of a business without renovating its values. The passage from one level to the next is nothing more than the onset of a transitional process, whereby *story changing*® is an indispensable vehicle to bring you and your staff to your destination.

(You will find more on *story changing*® in our books *D.R.E.A.M. of LEADERS*®. *Leadership is not an Illusion* and *Workbook: Responsibility.*) Employees must be guided through the transition. They must understand, for example, why consensus and dialog values have developed into a hierarchical structure value. Only then, will they join you on your way.

A few years ago, contrary to our emphatic recommendation, one of our clients converted his entire company structure from *Level 4* to *Level 6* — without *story changing*® or any other schooling. The board of directors believed it would suffice when each manager merely informed their employees of the undertaking. They did not want to roll out the transition, they chose to present the fait accompli. That was an error in judgment. Without properly preparing your workforce – the basis of your company – your plan is doomed. You cannot reconstruct your organigram overnight and hope everyone will applaud and join in whole-heartedly.

In the meantime, this company has launched a new attempt, better organized and with our support. Furthermore, the intended matrix organization will not be introduced to all departments, only in engineering and project management.

It is indeed feasible that organizational structures and their values vary from department to department within the same enterprise. The Sales and Marketing department could be built on *Level 3*, Finance on *Level 4* and Projects on *Level 5*. It goes to follow that Sales and Marketing need assertive values, while Financing requires stability and Projects demand flexibility, allowing fresh people-power to be shuttled in when there is a vacancy.

Above all, the process of realigning your organizational structure demands factoring in plenty of time and planning. Neglecting to do so is the major reason for transitional process failure. A few years ago, we led an international team in a workshop we call *Behavioral Controlling*, which deals with navigating group dynamics processes. This is best demonstrated by the values held, so we introduced the *9 Levels* model to the group. During the ensuing discussion, Tom, one of the participants, said, "If I have understood correctly, our company failed to move from level 4 to level 6 five years ago because we didn't sufficiently plan the process before launching it." "Exactly," we confirmed. "But that would also mean," Tom continued, "that a transitional process must be planned far in advance, since I have to clarify the values first or during planning." When we again confirmed his statement he shook his head, "How is that feasible in our high-speed times?" We responded with a counter question, "How successful are your transitional processes? Do they always proceed smoothly?" "Sometimes they do, sometimes they don't."

So, we began a collective retrospect, determining which of the past transitions were successfully carried out and which weren't. As it turned out, structural or process changes went well – primarily because the prevailing company values did need revising. In contrast, changes requiring modified values failed consistently. For example, the company, then on level 4, introduced a new IT system. Since level 4 means conformity, discipline and control, precisely the values needed for a new IT system, the transition was carried through without a hitch. But when it came to opening new markets, the company failed, since for such intentions the values must be remodeled. Often, organizational growth also demands values be adapted. Once a certain size or number of employees has been reached, an enterprise can no longer function at level 3, but necessitates a level 4 organizational structure.

Although Tom had understood us principally, he was not sold on the feasibility. "That may work in theory," he said, "All the same, with the day to day business demanding our full attention, we simply do not have the time to plan a transition so far in advance." "Are you listening to yourself?" we asked, with an intentionally provocative tone. "You admit you understand what we're talking about when we discover why past transitions have failed, but you're not willing to change your approach. Then, in maybe two years, when you once more attempt to tap new markets or target groups, your efforts will most likely come to naught. You will waste precious time, that you said yourself you do not have, on kneejerk planning. Yet, this approach costs you more time and energy than taking the bull by the horns from the start, prioritizing planning for a failsafe transition."

Our doubting Tom still wasn't convinced, so we approached him from another direction, "Have you ever heard the French adage, *Be patient – everything's difficult before it's easy.*" Tom laughed, "No, but there's a similar English expression – *Haste makes waste.* And that's a fact." Now, he's got it!

In the chapter *Sustainability* in our *Workbook: Responsibility* we pointed out that certain processes simply require time if they are to take root and grow. The same truth applies to adapting values in a company – you must work tirelessly, patiently and emphatically to successfully bring about change. Only then, can a transition succeed!

At the same time, you must also ask yourself if the values upheld in certain organizational structures are suitable for your business or your department. One such value is teamwork, for many companies an absolute must, even when it is not a viable approach. Such was the case with our client in northern Europe, where discovered that creating a team was not only impossible, it was also not practical. What they needed was a team-oriented group. What's the difference? you might ask. Well, a team works goal-oriented, everyone working toward the same end, each with a specific responsibility. In a group, on the other hand, each person has a different task or tasks that do not necessarily shoot for the same goal. Plainly put, every team member calls it a day at the same time. If one is finished, he offers his help to someone who isn't, until they are all ready to call it a day. A group member, however, works on his own assignment, so it's possible that one finishes up at 3pm, while another works until 8pm. That wouldn't happen with a team.

Our client in northern Europe dealt exclusively in distribution. Each employee worked a different market or product, so there were little or no interdependent activities. Thus, teamwork was neither sensible nor practicable. We therefore suggested a team-oriented group – the work itself was structured as a group effort, providing a sense of solidarity and group affiliation.

Difficulties arise when organizational structures are mickey-rigged around employee needs that are detrimental to business. Flexibility may work well and be beneficial on certain sectors, but a company's customer service simply cannot close at 1pm on Fridays because some workers have a private date. Customer service must also be accessible until at least 6pm during the week, if you don't want to frustrate and lose customers.

Another example illustrates how decisively values determine a person's behavior. Some years ago, we had a leader in one of our training programs who directed a home for mentally handicapped people. She was thoroughly annoyed when she was told she should introduce an annual employee talk and evaluation. She felt she had no right to judge another person and refused to comply with the new regulation, as it was wholly against her value system.

This example makes more than clear how difficult things become when varying values are not brought into sync. This is especially challenging for companies operating internationally. In our experience, Swedish corporate culture is commonly built around a level 6 organizational structure, i.e. non-hierarchal, based on consensus, dialog and cooperation. In other European countries, corporate culture moves primarily within level 3 orientation (eastern

Europe) or level 4 (southern and western Europe). Thus, decision-making approaches or leadership styles give rise to massive conflicts when these varying value systems collide. (More on decision-making in a global context can be found in our *Workbook: Responsibility* in the chapter *Making decisions*.)

Hence, a steadily progressive development to *Level 9* is, by the way, not necessarily mandatory. It would make no sense for a small craftsman's enterprise with 5 to 10 co-workers to ever go beyond *Level 2*. Essentially, the values must correspond with the surrounding structure. Even retroaction can be called for when circumstances demand it. There may be times when a company needs stability first and foremost, a phase which may be – within the same company – preceded or followed by a phase of assertiveness and aggressiveness.

**Key Lisciaman message**
Company values must be adapted to any alterations in a company's organizational structure. Only then will an enterprise endure. Such transitions must be carefully planned if they are to succeed for the long term.

**Your notes**

**Worksheet: Your company's values**

Which values are paramount to your enterprise?

Here is a list of values. Add values of your own that are not listed!

| | | | |
|---|---|---|---|
| Acceptance | Diligence | Modesty | Team spirit |
| Accuracy | Discipline | Neutrality | Thrift |
| Adventure | Effectiveness | Openness | Tolerance |
| Agility | Empathy | Recognition | Tradition |
| Altruism | Fairness | Reliability | Transparency |
| Assurance | Fidelity | Respect | Trust |
| Attentiveness | Freedom | Responsibility | |
| Brotherly love | Fun | Security | |
| Consideration | Helpfulness | Self-confidence | |
| Courage | Honesty | Sensitivity | |
| Decorum | Independence | Solicitude | |
| Determination | Innovation | Solidarity | |
| Dignity | Loyalty | Sustainability | |

How are your company's values applied to ...

a) the recruiting process?

_____

_____

_____

b) training new employees?

_____

_____

_____

c) promoting employees?

_____

_____

_____

d) releasing employees?

_____

_____

_____


Which areas show room for improvement? In which areas can you use your influence to ensure that company values are most strongly upheld?

_____

_____

_____

_____

_____

| | |
|---|---|
| *CEO:* | Not four weeks after a colleague was promoted it turns out that his former team is completely incompetent. |
| *LISCIA:* | What do you mean, incompetent? |
| *CEO:* | They're lost without him! Of course, that merely confirms that the team leader I promoted is an ace. But his team… |
| *LISCIA:* | What's your role in the team's failure? |
| *CEO:* | Mine? |
| *LISCIA:* | Yes. |
| *CEO:* | I obviously put my faith in the wrong people. |
| *LISCIA:* | Maybe. How well do you know this team? |
| *CEO:* | I know their key figures. |
| *LISCIA:* | The 'colleague' you promoted was obviously not quite ready to move on since his team still relied on him so heavily. As his leader, you bear the responsibility for not recognizing this. |
| *CEO:* | Oh. I never looked at it that way. |

## Making yourself superfluous

Paradoxical as it may sound, if you intend to be a successful leader, you must make yourself superfluous. You must bring your team or department so up to snuff, that your presence is no longer needed. Basically, it's all a matter of how you look at it. Here, the focus is not on the leader's laurels, but on the development and abilities of the people she leads.

It's a crying shame that so few leaders have yet to grasp that this, and only this, is their true quest.

When, during career coaching sessions, leaders ask us what the most failsafe path to the top could be, we tell them, "Make yourself superfluous." This statement is usually greeted with an incredulous shake of the head, "And then what? Then I'm no longer needed!" "Exactly," we reply, "and then you're ready to shape up another team."

Or, in other words, if a team needs permanent supervision, then their leader will never advance her career. Making yourself superfluous means making yourself open to new challenges.

This is reflected in the account of a young saleswoman at a large publishing house. During her first annual assessment with her boss, she was asked if she wished to advance her career at this establishment. The junior employee immediately answered with a firm "yes." Her supervisor, however, had one condition, "Beginning immediately, I will place two new colleagues under your care. When you have trained them to be just as proficient in sales as you are, we can make concrete plans for your promotion."

In response to the saleswoman's puzzled expression, her superior added, "You are an excellent saleswoman! A promotion, however, would pull you out of sales and into an unknown field, requiring the time and expense of developing and qualifying you for your new responsibilities. This is quite all right and part of the process. But I cannot afford two simultaneous works in progress, taking a loss in revenues. And that will inevitably be the case if you do not train your replacements beforehand."

The young saleswoman understood. If she didn't assume responsibility for the future of her current position, her career would stagnate. She had to make herself superfluous if she ever hoped to move up the career ladder.

For this reason, many companies carry out *Strategic Talent Reviews* on a regular basis. Here, leaders come together, usually every three months, to discuss potential successors for open or opening positions in the company. They differentiate between employees who are immediately ready for a new challenge and those who still need a year or two. In the latter cases, leaders consider what could accelerate potential candidates' preparedness for promotion, closing qualification gaps with targeted training and schooling.

Once more, in this context, values play a key role. When scouting for potential successors for a specific position in your company, be attentive to a candidate's values, as well as her qualifications. What we mean can be best illustrated with the following example. Imagine a company whose current sales manager, we'll call him Michael, upholds level 4 values – discipline, compliance, quality and a great deal of control. Company executives would like to take their business, including Michael, to level 5. Here, values such as advancement, company success, the introduction of key performance indicators, which naturally bring transparency to achieved successes. On level 5, the accent is not on a given employee's success. A person at home with level 5 values sees the big picture and her success is not necessarily at the cost of others.

In the *strategic talent review*, due to her abilities and talents, Anna was selected as Michael's potential successor. She represents level 3 values, i.e. is good with her elbows, is power-oriented and is basically interested in her own advancement. *Where* she advances is secondary.

No doubt, Anna's abilities put her in a position to succeed Michael, but her values are two steps away from the intended level 5. This aspect factors very rarely in companies' employee advancement since all attention is given to a candidate's professional qualifications, in the hopes of finding the optimal successor to successfully master new challenges.

Hence, company directors are faced with the following situation: Sales manager Michael should move from level 4 to level 5. He has found a qualified successor in Anna, but her values do not correspond to company strategy. Therefore, Michael must develop Anna to level 5, although he himself has not yet attained this level. We consider this ineffective. Much more efficient and goal-oriented is find a person who already encompasses the values desired. This person is either a member of the team or she must be taken from another department or another company altogether. Any lack of qualifications or skills can be easily transferred via schooling or training.

This does not mean that Anna is automatically disqualified for promotion to sales manager. It only means that her level 3 values are not appropriate for the European market. In China, however, she would be absolutely perfect, as the Chinese market requires assertiveness, power instincts and the ability to use your elbows. Thus, when applying a strategic talent review, you should first and foremost ascertain your candidate's values instead of limiting your view to abilities and competence.

Making yourself superfluous does not necessarily mean a move to another department or company. Nor does it compel you to take on a new team. Qualifying your subordinates and delegating certain responsibilities can also clear the way for other leadership duties, i.e. acquiring new customers or penetrating new markets. However, this can only be attained when your employees master everyday business procedures independently, only sporadically requiring your leadership input. Experience tells us many leaders deem themselves indispensable, the mere thought of becoming superfluous is intolerable. They are much more concerned with validating their existence than with the company's success. The HBDI® is an excellent tool to analyze this condition. (In our books *D.R.E.A.M. of LEADERS®. Leadership is not an Illusion* and *Workbook: Education* you will find a more detailed explanation of this personality profile method. This information, however, is not necessary to understand and work with this chapter.) A staff member with green preferences is hellbent on security. She will find it next to impossible to let go and transfer responsibility onto another.

Her colleague's rational, analytic blue preference, however, thoroughly understands the need to delegate, even though she lacks the necessary communication skills and empathy to do so elegantly. It principally comes down to leaders with red or yellow preference to best develop and qualify co-workers. And still, with their excessive sense of responsibility, these people may bond too strongly with their teams, making it emotionally difficult for them to cut the cord.

Thus, either several leaders must work together in close cooperation, or, alternatively, a leader's shortfalls must be schooled to supplement her inherent resources. We would approach this issue by guiding a leader with a blue and/ or green preference toward opening rational channels to *delegating* and *letting go*. While these skills are intrinsic to a person with yellow-red preferences – she instinctively acts accordingly – they do not come naturally to a blue-green leader. Therefore, together, we define precise motives and arguments, so a blue-green leader can rationally absorb why she should act as a yellow-red person would do.

A completely different example is that of a former client, CEO of a mid-sized enterprise, who wouldn't dream of making himself superfluous. He held his company in a dictatorial grip. He and he alone decided everything. His tyranny appalled competent employees by the dozen and absenteeism was rampant. Not so very long ago, the personnel developer called us with an inquiry, after we had already worked with the above-mentioned CEO. When we turned the HR manager down, she asked us why. We answered with the truth, "Because one of our essential principles states, *work must be fun*. And working for you is no fun at all."

This CEO and his leadership style were exasperating on several counts, but one particular event broke the camel's back. We had gathered for a briefing with the leader and several of his managers to decide on a concept. We presented our ideas and the CEO was thrilled, which pleased us to no end, at first. We turned to the sales director and personnel director, asking, "And what do you think?" Neither of them was given time to even draw breath, let alone respond, when the boss butted in, "You should know, Mr. Liscia, I will only establish democracy when my dictatorship becomes wearisome. We will implement your concept precisely as you suggested." We tried to catch his employees' eyes, but they were both gazing intently at the floor. Case closed.

This is a prime example of authoritative leadership at its best, or worst. The CEO may have had short-term financial success, but he also generated a work environment of fear and insecurity. In time, his attitude will inevitably bring about a fully demotivated workforce – excessive employee turnover and sick leave absenteeism were acute early warning symptoms.

For all intents and purposes, the consequences are catastrophic. In addition to a demotivated workforce, there wasn't a leader in the house who could remember making an independent decision. Literally everything passed over his highness's desk, no matter how miniscule. There wasn't a single area he did not have in his grasp. The concept of making himself superfluous was unthinkable. Should he be compelled to clear his desk overnight, it could mean the end of his business. His despotism had shaped a legacy of paralyzed and helpless employees, unable to act or decide autonomously.

Nearing the end of this chapter, we would like to recall an example of how quickly a person can realign his values when the right questions trigger reflection and insight. Or at least how she can focus on other values for a given time. Specifically, we are talking about Viktor, a sales director at a globally active IT enterprise. Viktor is responsible for two major clients in Europe. Viktor was more or less *commandeered* to us because his boss was concerned Viktor's obsessive non-stop work-load would eventually do damage to his health. Viktor finished his 35-hour week on Wednesday.

That meant, on Thursday he was going into round two. Our initial telephone conversation with Viktor's superior informed us that Viktor headed an eight-person team, and delegating tasks was not Viktor's strong point, to say the least. Although his team was perfectly capable of taking up the slack and then some, Viktor still did everything himself. Although the delegating issue was the catalyst for our work with Viktor, as you read on, you will see how this ties in with values.

In our first coaching session, Viktor confirmed the information we had already received from his boss. We also discovered that Viktor's co-workers were actually supposed to relieve him of certain tasks, but somehow, for assorted reasons, this didn't happen. To make a long story short, we discovered that Viktor did many things himself purely for the fun of it. He thoroughly enjoyed spending time with clients, sitting in the front row, being one of the 'guys.'

Viktor was a welcome and competent contact man and felt more like a colleague than a supplier. He was very proud of his official-unofficial status. Furthermore, Viktor is a salesman through and through, something he could only be among his customers and not as department manager behind a desk. He strove to win over his customers, fulfilling his profoundly personal ideal of a successful salesman.

We also posed this question for Viktor: What do you believe your prospects for moving further up the corporate ladder could be – specifically, from director to vice president – if you continue to be indispensable to your team and department. Indispensable, because he had not developed anyone in his department to take his place. This man, who treasured values such as pride, triumph, success and prestige, realized his behavior was his greatest hurdle if he wanted to move up in the company, attaining yet more status and prestige. He was called on to shift his focus toward letting go, toward his own and his employees' development and toward team spirit and reliability.

Coming back to the 9 Levels, Viktor must segue from being a one-man show, competitive and aggressive on level 3, to becoming team-strong and team-active, amid the clearly defined rules and assignments of level 4. Here, he will discover who is the best candidate for further development – fully in tune with level 5 – and, in time, be able to focus once more on his own career. Of course, this means work. But it also has a pleasant side-effect as Viktor is forced, albeit willingly so, to learn to delegate and to reduce his weekly work hours.

His employees feel increasingly valuable and appreciated since Viktor trusts them with more responsibility, launching a process lasting somewhat more than a year with most positive results.

**Key Lisciaman message**
Who really wants to be superfluous?
But should you want to advance your
career, it is essential to do just that.
Only those capable of letting go and
delegating will have the necessary
leeway to move onwards.

**Your notes**

## Worksheet: How do I make myself superfluous

Develop a plan for the next 12 months, aiming to make yourself superfluous to your team or department!

Consider the following thoughts and include them in your plan:
1. Who has the most potential to replace me (in-house or external)?

_____

_____

_____

_____

2. How and by whom can this person be developed to take my place?

_____

_____

_____

_____

3. Which gap would this person leave in the team (when an in-house employee) when she/he takes over my position, and how can this gap be filled?

_____

_____

_____

_____

4. How will the other team members react to their new superior?

_____

_____

_____

_____

5. Where do I want to go now?

_____
_____
_____
_____
_____

6. What am I leaving behind (fond friends, habits, hassles, etc.)?

_____
_____
_____
_____
_____

7. How do I have to develop myself in preparation for the position I want to assume?

_____
_____
_____
_____
_____

8. What is the first step toward the new position?

_____
_____
_____
_____

9. When will I take this step?

_____
_____
_____
_____

| | |
|---|---|
| *CEO:* | We do our best to meet our employees' needs so that everyone is satisfied with their work situation. And yet, according to our latest employee survey, satisfaction is at an all-time low. |
| *LISCIA:* | How is your workforce structured? |
| *CEO:* | Our staff mainly consists of experts. Early on, we insisted on a comprehensive education, with or without a university diploma. This applies to our oldest employees, who have been with us 20 years or more, and is still a prerequisite today. So, our structure is pretty much homogenous. |
| *LISCIA:* | Homogenous in the sense of globally active with an age span from 25 to 60 years, as your homepage states? |
| *CEO:* | Yes, that is – wait a sec. |
| *LISCIA:* | Your company is composed of employees from 5 distinct cultures and 3 different generations. That's not exactly homogenous. |
| *CEO:* | You think that's the reason for the poor survey results? |
| *LISCIA:* | Let's call it the indiscriminate, therefore inapplicable, definition of your workers' needs that takes its toll. |

## Intercultural, virtual and cross-generational teams

Nowadays, a single-nation business is a rare thing indeed. Even smallish, mid-sized companies often develop global or international strategies, including craft businesses. For corporations, it's par for the course. Yet the moment a company opens a location out of the country, the challenges grow accordingly, regardless of the enterprise's size and workforce.

Like with one of our clients. His mid-sized automobile supplier company employs 250 workers and belongs to a concern with a total of 1,600 employees and production plants in the U.S.A., Mexico and China, among others. Accordingly, our client occasionally works on projects with multi-national colleagues. All in a day's work for globally active enterprises.

A global leader heading an international, multi-cultural team is presented with a wealth of approaches, knowledge and skills to draw from, enriching the joint effort.

In order to tap this wealth, communication hurdles need to be gracefully cleared. The leader may have all her co-workers at the ready, but as they come from all corners of the Earth, they bring their cultures and languages with them.

A successful leader in one culture does not necessarily make him a successful leader in another, unfamiliar culture.

"Although you may have been a very successful leader in your own culture, if you hope to motivate and engage people around the globe, you will need a multi-faceted approach. Today it's no longer enough to know how to lead the Dutch way or the Mexican way, the American way or the Chinese way. You must be informed enough and flexible enough to choose which style will work best in which cultural context and then deliberately decide how to adapt (or not) to get the results you need."[1]

If you have already read our *Workbook Responsibility*, you may remember the chapter *Making decisions*. Here, we talked about how important it is for global leaders to take international dimensions into account when making decisions, i.e. who in a given culture decides what on which basis. The same thing applies to other areas, such as communication. Of course, communication is the key to all phases of teamwork, but forms and styles of cultural expression vary enormously.

"... at the outset, a leader must tactfully mediate to prevent misinterpretations of cultural customs. People of an individualistic culture (i.e. U.S.A.) are more apt to express their own opinion as someone from a collectivistic culture (i.e. China). [...] Emotional expressions also have many faces. Japanese, for example, often smile when they are angry."[2]

Working with virtual teams, with team members scattered all over the globe instead of together in one place, heightens the challenge. Compounding difficulties is the fact that you are leading people you hardly know or don't know at all and any meetings that may take place entail travel. This is all quite doable, as long as the leader has the appropriate attitude, is aware of the consequences and consciously shoulders the responsibility.

Otherwise, there is the risk of falling back on purely managerial tactics since virtual teams make great claims on a global leader's soft skills. Without being able to read body language messages, he must be adept at reading or listening

---

[1]   Harvard Business Review, *Being the Boss in Brussels, Boston, and Beijing*, July-August 2017

[2]   wiwo.de, Global Management. *So führen Sie internationale Teams / Leading international teams*, 01.05.2014

between the lines. Even video conferences depict only a fraction of the whole picture. He must also be extremely flexible in adapting to foreign values or cultures.

Some time ago, we were coaching a program manager who was guiding an international project. His team members were in Mexico, Hungary and China. Time differences made it impossible to hold collective telephone or video conferences, which meant twice as many meetings. Hence, there were few meetings with all team members simultaneously. The circumstances wreaked havoc with the leader's time-management, which in turn heavily taxed his stress-management. He knew directly upon launching the project, that it would be more than just a challenge; it could become a tribulation.

In this context, digital leadership plays an increasingly significant role. After all, it was digitalization that made global leadership possible in the first place. Thanks to electronic media, the same office or even time zone no longer needs to be shared in order for leaders and employees to work together successfully.

"Digitalization has not only changed the demands on leaders, it has also opened his options for shaping his leadership. As a rule, however, you must design your leadership method yourself. It makes no difference which tools you use – digital platforms or international guidelines – what you must have is the ability to lead, be it analogue or digital."[1]

Should a leader not possess the necessary digital knowledge, a company may need to take on an expert in the field, such as a Chief Information Officer (CIO), Chief Digital Officer (CDO) or Chief Technology Officer (CTO). Our digital achievements not only influence how we work, but also how we lead.

"One of the key digital leadership elements (according to Creusen) is the further development of participative leadership models, targeting increased speed, agility and flexibility in decision-making processes."[2]

These are the demands a global leader must be prepared to meet. They have little to do with the fairy-tale images so many people still carry around in their

---

[1]  zeit.de, *"Chefs werden auch in Zukunft nicht überflüssig". Die Digitalisierung verändert die Arbeitswelt / The future still needs bosses, digitalization changes the working world.*, 12.12.2014

[2]  https://de.wikipedia.org/wiki/Digital_Leadership (not available in English)

heads, where everyone adores everyone, working passionately and harmoniously on a project that not only runs perfectly, but is finished before the deadline – the sweet, happy end from the best of Hollywood.

In reality, virtual team members are more like puzzle pieces scattered all over the world. You fervently hope they fit together in the end and the picture is complete, but there is no guarantee that this will happen. How can it, when you hardly know each other, not to mention rarely see each other? Video conferences are no tremendous help either since the greater part of daily communications ensues via email. We often hear in coaching sessions that the lack of personal contact triggers conflicts that can easily escalate. If the team could meet in person, fermenting problems could be discussed and solved before they begin to seethe, nipping discord in the bud.

Another contemporary leadership liability arises from cross-generational teams – sometimes four different generations working on the same project. A team encompassing Baby Boomers (1946-1964), Generation X (1965-1979), Generation Y (1980-1994), and Generation Z (1995 onwards) furnishes the team structure with four different value systems, perspectives and expectations, as well as quadrophonic communication styles. This can quickly lead to tension and controversy. For leaders, this is a new frontier. Once, it was societal influence that shaped a generation and evolution took it's time bringing about change. Today, our technical progress shapes the coming generations, shortening the timespan between them, while simultaneously stamping each new generation with distinct identities and value systems. It's a powder keg looking for a lit match.

Leaders must be prepared for this situation, once they have done the necessary research. The focus is currently held on Millennials or Generation y, employees born between 1980 and 1995. In our books *D.R.E.A.M. of LEADERS®. Leadership is not an Illusion* and *Workbook: Responsibility* we gave a brief description of this situation. Generation Y highly values flexible work hours and job rotation, while fusing their professional lives and leisure time. On the whole, companies have adapted to these needs and demands. However, in the meanwhile, Generation Z, those born after 1995, is champing at the bit or has already joined the global workforce. Many employers have yet to realize that this younger generation is bringing their own set of new and different challenges.

"Christian Scholz from the University of Saarland [...] observed: 'Mindset and attributes of these young people is completely different than that of Generation Y.' According to Scholz, Generation Z has a whole new professional identity. There is little interest in blending professional and personal areas of their lives. Today's youth have well observed how often Generation Y brings their work home with them and are literally chained to their laptops. 'Gen Z wants regular work hours, open-end contracts and clearly defined structures at work,' employment experts tell us."[1]

Thus, companies are now called on to wholly rethink their own structures and adapt their leadership strategy as well as their leadership culture to the new generation. If Gen Z needs security, predictability, structure and reliability, then it's no wonder that the gastronomy and hotel sectors are wringing their hands over the lack of trainees. In both fields, it is common for employees to be semi-permanently on call, which is diametrically opposed to the needs of Generation Z. Recruiting departments must then adapt and possibly even reorganize in-house processes.

Observing these leadership challenges when it comes to intercultural, virtual and cross-generational teams, you become more than aware of the multifarious burdens contemporary leaders are expected to bear. It is not enough to be subject-specifically prepared. Leaders absolutely must be equipped to consciously handle physical and mental resources – an issue we address in detail in our books *D.R.E.A.M. of LEADERS®. Leadership is not an Illusion* and *Workbook: Responsibility.*

---

[1]  welt.de, *Was Generation Z vom Berufsleben erwartet / What Generation Z expects from their professional life*, 06.03.2016

**Key Lisciaman message**
Heterogeneous teams are an enormous
challenge for leaders. He must possess
excellent instincts, be flexible and have
the knowledge necessary to lead these
teams successfully.

## Your notes

**Worksheet: Who is on your team?**

How many team members are ...

Gen Z?            _____        number of women  _____        number of men  _____
(1995 onwards)

Gen Y?            _____        number of women  _____        number of men  _____
(1980 - 1994)

Gen X?            _____        number of women  _____        number of men  _____
(1965 - 1979)

Babyboomer?  _____        number of women  _____        number of men  _____
(1946 - 1964)


Which nationalities are represented on your team?

_____        _____
_____        _____
_____        _____
_____        _____


How many team members do you lead virtually (telephone, video conference, in writing)?

_____
_____
_____


What challenges do you face in leading your team constellation?

_____
_____
_____

How have you handled these challenges thus far?

_____

_____

_____

Which hurdles have you circumvented up to now?

_____

_____

_____

_____

What are the consequences of your avoidance?

_____

_____

_____

_____

What knowledge do you need to approach such hurdles with confidence?

_____

_____

_____

_____

How can you attain this knowledge?

_____

_____

_____

_____

| | |
|---|---|
| *CEO:* | Whenever I look ahead, all I can see is a bottomless pit. |
| *LISCIA:* | Try looking down instead of ahead, what's on the other side of the abyss? |
| *CEO:* | Chaos. |
| *LISCIA:* | That's the abyss. What comes after the abyss? |
| *CEO:* | I can't see that far. |
| *LISCIA:* | How were things three years ago? |
| *CEO:* | Even worse. Compared to back then, I'm in paradise. |
| *LISCIA:* | Describe what it was like three years ago. |
| *CEO:* | We were on the brink of bankruptcy. |
| *LISCIA:* | And today? |
| *CEO:* | Today we're doing really well. |
| *LISCIA:* | When was the last time you were grateful for today? |
| *CEO:* | Grateful? With all this chaos coming at me? |
| *LISCIA:* | Forget the bottomless pit for a minute! Where's the gratitude surrounding you right this second? You saved your company from ruin! How does that feel? |
| *CEO:* | Good. |
| *LISCIA:* | That's a beginning. |

## Just be happy

Happiness is also attitude-business. It is a matter of accepting the status quo – an essential building block to happiness, in our opinion. This has nothing to do with resigning to your fate. No, it is about truly accepting things you cannot change, no matter what you do. It makes no sense to cry over spilled milk, brooding only feeds the fire of negativity, while making it impossible to let go of the past and move ahead. A terrible waste of time.

The British say, "Love it, change it or leave it." But not every co-worker has the luxury to change things, particularly during transitional processes. Depending on her position in the hierarchy, she can influence decisions or not. When she can't, her only choice is to bite the bullet, either love it or leave it. She must decide how she will deal with the situation for her future. Mourning the past will get her nowhere.

When she does look back, she should keep her eyes on the positive aspects, the *reverse gap*, i.e. the period during which she was successful or overcame difficulties.

Many people focus their attention on the future. This is basically a good thing, but also entails putting off happiness, treating it as a reward – reaped sometime in the future – for deeds well done. We frequently hear such statements like, "When I retire I will have more time for my family." Or, "Let me finish this project first, then I'll relax."

The problem is, this approach keeps us from actually attaining our just rewards. The moment they are in reach, we take on another task, pushing the longed-for respite or pleasurable event further into the future. This is called a *future gap*, the time between the present moment and the future reward. And it explains why we are perpetually dissatisfied. Happy today? No, but maybe tomorrow, when I have done this, that and the other thing. I might have moments of satisfaction, but happy I am not.

We prefer to look at the *reverse gap* before setting new goals for the future. We review the last 2, 3 or 4 years, asking, what is better now? What has changed for the better during this time? What makes you happy now? What made you happy then? Focusing on the positive past, you experience happiness. You are proud of and satisfied with yourself.

When planning your future gap, you will automatically include the things that turned up in your reverse gap – that which made you happy in the past and wish to take with you into the future. Naturally, you want to achieve your goals, but they may not be so high flying as they once were. And that's the whole point, your happiness is also part of the plan, integrated into the space between goal and reward, closing the gap.

This model works particularly well with people who have recognizably evolved in a positive direction. All the same, even disastrous strokes of fate may, in retrospect, have their positive attributes. You may have a few scars to tell the tale, but you also now know who your faithful friends are and on whom you can rely. Negative experiences can certainly turn out to be valuable, when they serve to make you stronger. Perhaps, later on, you might just realign your priorities; placing less weight on accrued wealth, a luxurious lifestyle and higher status, and focusing more on the life-lessons learned.

Ever since the extreme athlete Joey Kelly spoke at our *Think Tank* in October 2016 – and again at our February 2018 *Think Tank* – giving profoundly fascinating lectures on his experience with endurance sports and his time with the Kelly Family, we have been following his career and that of his family with interest.

During the 1990s, the Kelly Family played in front of capacity audiences in mega-venues, selling several million recordings. Upon their father's death in 2002, the family fell apart, the millions were lost, and the brothers and sisters split up, each going their separate ways for the most part. Later on, independently of one another, each retold the perils of their popularity; the intense pressure, the loss of privacy, the limited freedom, and the overall burden, as most of them were still very young at the time. Still, music remained an important aspect in their lives, some successfully launching solo careers. This time around, though, they wanted to leave the nineties behind and go back to the roots. The Kelly Family began as buskers.

In his book *Streetkid: Fluch und Segen, ein Kelly zu sein / The Curse and Blessing of Being a Kelly*, Jimmy Kelly explained his motivation.

"I certainly didn't want to go back into show business. I'd seen enough to know that all that glitters, is not gold. [...] I wanted to get away from all that superficial glamour and tinsel. [...] I had long felt the desire to return to the street, where I had been happy. [...] Usually, you only come back to fundamental desires when the surrounding circumstances change drastically. Who would leave their comfort zone voluntarily? [...] Every time an athlete suffers defeat, he immediately returns to basic training, again and again. Monks constantly return to the source of devotion. The Kelly Family was originally a grass root band, playing for the people. So, I thought, if I could earn enough on the street to support my family, I would have won back a bit of happiness."[1]

His brother Angelo followed a similar path:

"To support his family, [...] he began playing music on the street again – just as he had done in his childhood. Angelo Kelly describes the time they lived in a trailer as intense but happy. Between 2011 and 2014, the family rambled around in Spain, Italy, France and Denmark [...]. His wife taught their children while Angelo went busking in the pedestrian zones. [...] It's all about the simple

---

[1]   Kelly, Jimmy, Streetkid: *Fluch und Segen, ein Kelly zu sein / The Curse and Blessing of Being a Kelly*, Heyne Verlag 2017, S. 11f.

life, family bonds and the joy of making music."[1] Both Jimmy and his brother Angelo made use, although perhaps subconsciously, of the *reverse gap*. They turned their attention to what had worked well in the past, to that which made them happy.

These insights made it possible for them to plan and shape a future of fulfillment (*future gap*). They could happily forego the hype surrounding them in the nineties, and the lack of privacy they suffered back then was definitely not going to happen again – they just wanted to make music, and nothing more. After a long break, the Kelly Family, down to six active members, once more gave concerts in larger venues. Angelo, however, had learned from the past, he would only play larger gigs. "…when we do so in a way that is healthy for all of us."[2]

Last year, during our junior employee program, we carried out a gap analysis with Jessica, a young leader. It was immediately clear to us that she was very eager to investigate the *reverse gap*. What really surprised us, though, were the results of her written analysis. After giving it plenty of thought, Jessica concluded she would give up her good and promising position in a pharmaceutical company and join her husband in the family business he had taken over from his father five years ago. Between finishing her studies and beginning her professional life, Jessica had worked in the business for three months and enjoyed it immensely. Even then, she had considered staying there and turning down the pharmaceutical company's offer. "But my husband and I thought it would be unreasonable to throw such a well-paid, promising career opportunity out the window." Jessica wrote. "At least one of us should have a secure job, in case the family business didn't work out." Yet, there it stood, healthy and in need of her qualities. And to be honest, her current position did not bring the hoped-for fulfillment. This had nothing to do with the company, her salary and certainly not with her wonderful team – it just wasn't the right place for her, that certain something was missing. Jessica was so happy when the gap analysis gave her clarity and direction.

---

[1]  stern.de, *Angelo Kellys Auswandererfamilie bringt Quotenrekord / Angelo Kelly's Expat Family Breaks Viewer Quotas*, 18.05.2016

[2]  Ibid.

Closing the gap also means enjoying the moment. It means acknowledging the positive events in your life, no matter how small they may be. During our self-management coaching sessions and seminars, we recommend keeping a Book of Happiness. Every evening, before going to bed, write down five good things that made you happy that day. Pay extra attention to the tiny things; a smile from the supermarket cashier, your favorite song on the radio or a pat on the back from your boss.

Most participants have a tough time getting into the swing of it in the beginning but sticking with it eventually brings the desired results. Something nice happens to you and you immediately think, "This is one for my Book of Happiness!" You no longer need to comb through your entire day to find the positive events, you experience happiness the moment pleasant things happen. Your perception has changed focus, from a negative or neutral attitude, you have become positive. Consciously perceiving and taking pleasure in small events is simply a question of attentiveness. A Book of Happiness also has the advantage of sending you to sleep with positive thoughts, giving your subconscious something nice to work with.

In her feedback on one of our workshops, one participant – let's call her Felicia – wrote that it was her Book of Happiness that made her aware of how often she began her day with negative thoughts. This changed once she began consistently – every evening – to write down five good things that happened that day. "It wasn't long at all before I started waking up with a much more positive attitude," she wrote. Apparently, her subconscious quickly latched onto her focus on pleasant events. Felicia also discovered she could magnify the positive influence, what she called *doubling the effect*. Each morning, she recalled the positive events she had written down the evening before, which, she wrote to us, helped her greet the new day with even more positive energy and momentum.

Your Book of Happiness is an equally supportive tool when things are not going so well. When all you can see are the wrong turns and poor judgments, a look in your Book of Happiness shows you another reality, turning your attention back to the basic pleasures in your life.

If you wish to redirect your focus, giving more attention to the present moment and positive events, get started right away with our Book of Happiness! You will find more information in this book's appendix.

**Key Lisciaman message**
There's no secret to or magic formula for boosting your happiness. Acceptance, a good attitude and certain techniques can distinctly increase your sense of happiness!

## Your notes

46

**Worksheet: Have a look at your reverse gap!**

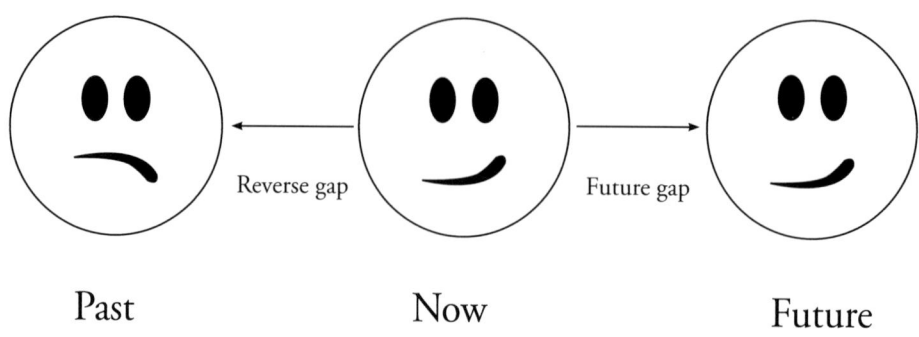

Past                          Now                          Future

1. What makes you happy now, when you compare it with the past?

_____

_____

2. What has changed for the better?

_____

_____

3. What have you achieved (for you, your family, your partner, your company) that makes you proud and happy?

_____

_____

4. If things have not improved over the years, then ask yourself what you can learn from past experiences to help you shape a better future.

_____

_____

_____

_____

Now look at your future gap!

1. Where do you want to go?

_____

_____

_____

_____

_____

2. What's the attraction?

_____

_____

_____

_____

_____

3. What should be different than today in the future?

_____

_____

_____

_____

_____

4. What can you learn from your past and apply to your future?

_____

_____

_____

_____

**The Authors**

Marcello, Gianni and Jan Liscia (left to right)

Since its inception in 2000, taking shape in Paderborn, Germany, the name *Liscia Consulting* has gained ground on both national and international terrain with their excellent work in leader development. A most competent partner for strategy, conception and getting things done.

Business leaders Gianni, Marcello and Jan Liscia are not your everyday seminar conductors. Nor are they generic trainers or coaches. Gianni, Marcello and Jan Liscia are consultants who train and coach *leaders*. They are strategic partners, guiding and mediating transitional processes.

**www.Liscia-Consulting.com**

## Keynote presentations for your event

On the pulse of change with inspiring keynote lectures! A keynote presentation can be designed to run 30 minutes or up to 3 hours – according to your event's agenda!

Together, we determine the focus of your D.R.E.A.M. of LEADERS® keynote lecture, i.e. Employee Engagement in Global Leadership, Transitional Process Leadership or Digital Leadership. Our multifarious and unusual approach infuses your business with new impulses, creating an atmosphere of awakening and a desire for change.

A rational/emotional composition coupled with the blunt, stark reality of our times invokes profound reflection. To easier digest discomfiting truth, we served it with a healthy portion of humor.

**www.Liscia-Consulting.com**

## One 'n' Herman, the artist

Herman, illustrator

Herman is, and has been for some time, one of the most high-profile, successful pop art painters of our time. His edgy, idiosyncratic graphics and pictures are downright bodacious. Once a trained screen printer, his unleashed creativity has astonished viewers at over 200 national and international exhibits. Herman has been an independent artist since 1991.

Over the past years, the name Herman can also be found under cartoons drawn for a variety of German publishing houses. His *flying heart* comic strip in *Bravo*, a German youth magazine, was published several consecutive years, becoming a household name. The same can be said of the 18 Herman collector's glasses commissioned by *Ritzenhoff*. In 2007, bids were made for 49 Herman paintings at a charity auction benefiting the Peter Maffay Foundation.

**www.Kuenstler-Herman.de**

**Want more? Here's an overview of all books**
**by Gianni, Jan & Marcello Liscia:**

Gianni, Jan & Marcello Liscia

# D.R.E.A.M.
# of
# LEADERS

Leadership is not an Illusion

Illustrations:
Herman Reichold

ISBN: 978-3-744-88271-2 – 19,90 € (D), E-Book: 14,99 € (D)

Gianni, Jan & Marcello Liscia

# WORKBOOK
# DEDICATION

Dedication to the work at hand, with heart and soul,
24 hours a day

Illustrations:
Herman Reichold

ISBN: 978-3-7528-5787-0 – 8,90 € (D), E-Book: 4,99 € (D)

Gianni, Jan & Marcello Liscia

# WORKBOOK
# RESPONSIBILITY

Showing responsibility for decisions made, for employees
and for oneself

Illustrations:
Herman Reichold

ISBN: 978-3-7528-5825-9 – 8,90 € (D), E-Book: 4,99 € (D)

Gianni, Jan & Marcello Liscia

# WORKBOOK
# EDUCATION

Personal and employee education

Illustrations:
Herman Reichold

ISBN: 978-3-7528-5826-6 – 8,90 € (D), E-Book: 4,99 € (D)

Gianni, Jan & Marcello Liscia

# WORKBOOK
# MOTIVATION

Being ready to perform is the basis for all action

Illustrations:
Herman Reichold

ISBN: 978-3-7528-5828-0 – 8,90 € (D), E-Book: 4,99 € (D)

Gianni, Jan & Marcello Liscia

# The Book of Happiness

A work and reflection diary

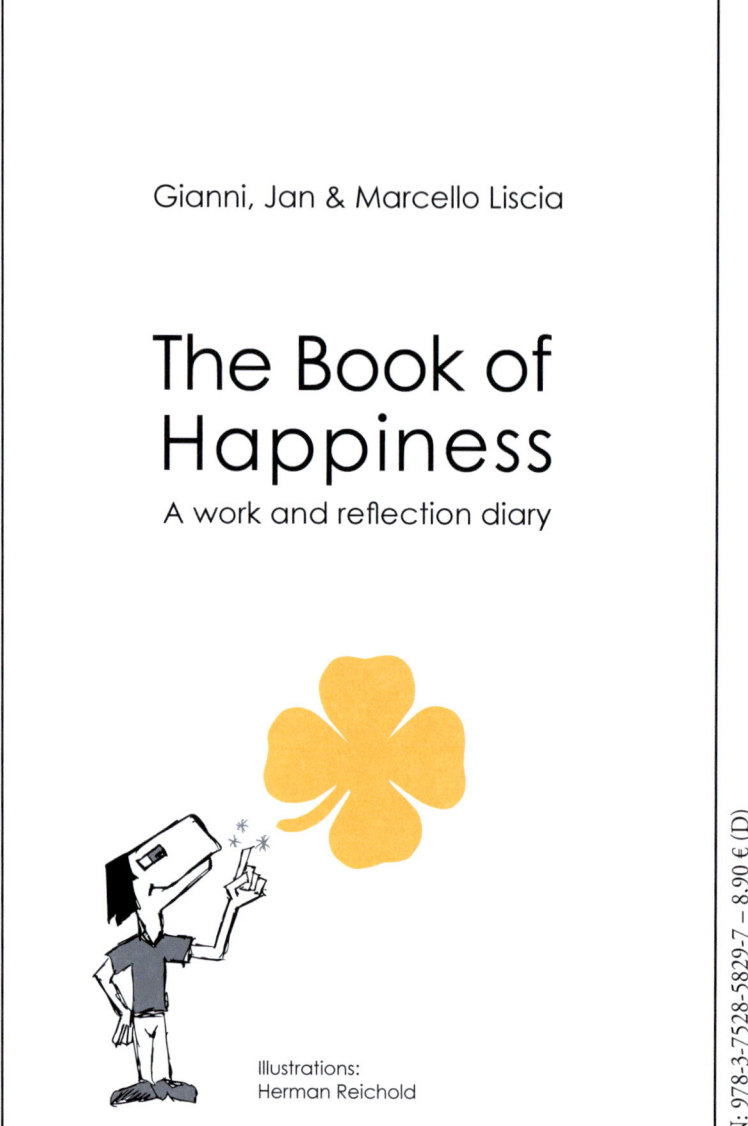

Illustrations:
Herman Reichold

ISBN: 978-3-7528-5829-7 – 8,90 € (D)

**All of our titles are available as ebooks (except The Book of Happiness) and can be enjoyed in the German language, too!**